MW00928086

The Old Fasl

Gags and Funny Stories
in the Classic Stand-Up Style

Compiled by Hugh Morrison

Montpelier Publishing

London

2015

ISBN-13: 978-1514261989

ISBN-10: 1514261987

Published by Montpelier Publishing, London.

Printed by Amazon Createspace.
This edition copyright © 2015. All rights reserved.

A fat man wanted to lose weight so he went to the doctor who made him stand on the scales. The man sucked his tummy in. 'That won't help you,' said the doctor. 'Yes it will,' said the man, 'I can see the numbers now.'

Husband: Darling, will you still love me when I'm old, fat and balding?

Wife: I do.

A hysterical woman burst into the office of a hypnotherapist.

'Doctor, you must help me!' she cried. 'I've been faithful to my husband for twenty five years, but last night I slept with a complete stranger. I feel so guilty – you must hypnotise me so that I forget all about it!'

The doctor sighed and said 'not you again...'

'Why did you dump your girlfriend?'

'She kept using four letter words.'

'Is that so bad?'

'It is if they're words like "stop,", "don't", "can't", and "won't".'

'There's nothing really wrong with you,' said the doctor to his patient. 'Just drink a glass of this tonic each night followed by a hot bath and you'll be right as rain.' The next day the doctor returned to check on the man who looked worse than ever. 'Did you drink the tonic?' asked the doctor. 'Yes,' said the man, 'but I could only manage half the hot bath.'

My wife and I celebrated our tenth wedding anniversary by going back to the hotel we spent our honeymoon night in. Only this time, it was me who stayed in the bathroom and cried!

Doctor: There's nothing wrong with you. You'll live to be sixty.

Patient: I AM sixty!

Doctor: See, what did I tell you!

Farmer Giles wanted to buy his neighbour's cow, but on enquiring the price he was shocked to learn it was £50.

'What', he protested, 'here I am, your friend and neighbour, and you ask a price like that?'

'I'll tell you what', replied the other farmer, 'seeing you are my neighbour I'll give you 20% discount.'

Now Farmer Giles was not much of a scholar and he wasn't quite sure what this meant so he said 'I'll think about it.'

He went off down the road and was still trying to figure it out when he saw the local school-mistress coming towards him on her bicycle. He beckoned her to stop and said

'Now tell me, Miss Smith, if I were to offer you £50, less 20% discount, what would you take off?'

Miss Smith thought for a moment and then declared 'Everything, except my ear-rings.'

'Have you ever had an ex-girlfriend you can't get rid of?'

'Yes – my wife.'

Sir Winston Churchill is said to have attended a banquet where he sat next to a Methodist minister with strict views on temperance. A waitress offered Sir Winston a glass of wine, who took one, and then moved on to the minister. 'Young lady,' said the clergyman in a shocked voice, 'I would rather commit adultery than drink alcohol.' Sir Winston called to the waitress, 'Come back - I didn't realise there was a choice!'

Smith: How did you get on at the doctor?

Jones: Bad news I'm afraid. I've got to take a tablet every day for the rest of my life.

Smith: That doesn't sound too bad, what are you worried about?

Jones: He only gave me three tablets!

'I'll never forget the day of my wife's funeral. There was a huge crowd and we sang 'Abide with Me'.

'It sounds like a lovely service.'

'Oh, I didn't go to the service, it was Cup Final day.'

'Doctor, I'm thinking of getting a vasectomy.'

'That's a big decision. Have you discussed it with your family?'

'Yes, we took a vote, and they're in favour of it 15 to 2.'

Patient: I keep dreaming that beautiful women are throwing themselves at me, but that I keep pushing them away.

Doctor: Well, what do you want me to do about it?

Patient: Break my arm.

An American tourist arrived at Heathrow and got into a taxi. Just outside the airport the taxi stopped at a Pelican crossing. The tourist heard the sound of the crossing signal and asked the driver, 'hey buddy, what's that beeping noise?'

'That's so that blind people know when the lights are green,' said the driver.

'My God,' cried the American. 'You mean they let blind people drive here?'

An alcoholic, a compulsive eater and a hypochondriac were sitting in a doctor's waiting room.

'I'm so tired and thirsty, I must have a glass of whisky,' said the alcoholic.

'I'm so tired and thirsty, I must have a double milk shake,' said the compulsive eater.

'I'm so tired and thirsty,' said the hypochondriac, 'I must have diabetes.'

Magistrate (to defendant): You've been brought here for drinking.

Defendant: OK, then let's get started!

What's the easiest way to add insult to injury? Write something rude on a plaster cast.

McTavish: How was that Caribbean cruise ye won in that competition?

McGregor: Terrible. For the first three days I didnae eat a thing.

McTavish: Seasick?

McTavish: No, I didn't realise the meals were included free.

My wife said to me 'you'll drive me to my grave.' I had the car ready in two minutes.

My mother in law says she'll dance on my grave. It doesn't bother me, I'm getting buried at sea.

A man was squeezed into the narrow back seat of a small taxi, with his very fat wife.

'I bet you wish you'd married a slimmer woman!' she joked.

'I did,' he replied.

Cohen and Goldberg were crossing the English Channel in a ferry when a huge storm blew up. The boat was pitched and tossed about like a toy as the waves crashed over the decks. Cohen clutched Goldberg and said 'I'm terrified the ship's going to sink!' 'Why worry already?' said Goldberg. 'Is it *your* ship?'

People who work on make-up counters are so smug about their jobs. They're always rubbing it in customers' faces.

'My wife's one of twins.'

'How can you tell them apart?'

'Her brother's got a moustache.'

'My wife says I'm a chauvinist pig who thinks a woman's place is in the kitchen.'

'Why don't you buy her something to make her feel more appreciated. What's her favourite flower?'

'Self-raising, I think.'

A conjuror was performing on a cruise ship. After the first trick, a heckler shouted 'It's up your sleeve!' The conjuror was annoyed but carried on to his next trick. 'It's under the table!' yelled the heckler. This went on for several more tricks until suddenly, the ship's boiler exploded. Half an hour later the conjuror and the heckler were clinging to some wreckage in the sea. The heckler said 'Alright, I give up. What did you do with the ship?'

'My new car's got everything. Alloys, turbo charge, bucket seats, and GPS over-ride.'

'What on earth's a GPS over-ride?'

'My wife.'

A married couple were sitting on the sofa sipping wine. Out of the blue, the wife said 'I love you.'

'Is that you or the wine talking?' asked the husband.

'It's me,' replied the wife. 'Talking to the wine.'

'That's a nice new locket. Is there some sort of memento inside?

'A lock of my husband's hair.'

'But he's still alive!'

'Yes, but his hair is gone.'

Tramp (to businessman): Lend me a tenner until payday, guv?

Businessman: Hmm, when's payday?

Tramp: How should I know? You're the one with a job!

'If I were to die first,' said a woman to her husband, 'would you ever marry again?'

'Well...I suppose it's possible.' replied the man.

'And would you live in this house?'

'Can't see why not.'

'And would you sleep in our bed?'

'No point buying a new one.'

'I bet you'd even let her wear my clothes, wouldn't you?'

'No, she's smaller than you.'

A woman was in the kitchen frying some eggs when her husband came up beside her.

'Not too much gas, dear, turn it down a bit....flip the eggs over now, quickly, or they'll stick...move them round the pan more, or the edges will go all brown...watch out for that grease on the side of the pan! Turn off the gas now – turn it off! Turn it off! Hurry up or they'll be burnt!'

'What on earth is wrong with you?' said his wife.

'Nothing,' replied the husband calmly. 'I just wanted to show you what it feels like when I'm driving.'

A man was with his wife in a romantic restaurant.

'Darling, you look wonderful in this candlelight,' he said to her.

'Oh darling. That's such a sweet thing to say,' she replied.

'Yes,' said the man. 'We'll have to get some candles at home.'

'All my husband and I do is argue. I'm so worried about it, I've lost at least half a stone.'

'Why don't you just leave him?'

'I'd like to lose another half a stone first.'

'If I had a rabbit in a hutch, and I bought another rabbit, how many rabbits would I have?'

'Why, two, of course'

'No, ten.

'You don't know your arithmetic'

'You don't know my rabbits.'

A man went into a restaurant and said to the waiter, 'I'll have the tomato soup, the roast beef with gravy, and the apple crumble and custard.' 'Why sir,' replied the waiter, 'how do you know we serve all that? You haven't even looked at the menu.' 'No,' replied the man, 'but I've looked at the tablecloth.'

My wife went to the beauty parlour and got a mud pack. She looked great for three days – then the mud fell off.

A man who compromises when he's wrong is wise; a man who compromises when he's right is married.

Wife: I want a boob job.

Husband: What's wrong with the job you've got?

Smith: If it wasn't for that moustache you'd look just like my wife.

Jones: I haven't got a moustache.

Smith: No, but my wife has.

A religious young lady came home from a date, rather sad. She told her mother, 'John proposed to me an hour ago.'

'Then why are you so sad?' her mother asked.

'Because he also told me he was an atheist. Mother, he doesn't even believe there's a hell.'

Her mother replied, 'Marry him anyway. Between the two of us, we'll show him how wrong he is.'

Wife (to husband): We're not going to Spain on holiday again. The climate disagrees with mother.

Husband: That must be the bravest climate in the world!

A father left work a little late one night and, while on his way home, he remembered that he had not yet purchased a Christmas gift for his little daughter. He dashed into a toy shop and asked the assistant, 'How much is the Barbie doll in the window?'

The assistant replied, 'We have "Barbie goes to the gym" for £19.95, "Barbie plays Golf" for £19.95, "Barbie goes Shopping" for £19.95, "Barbie goes to the Beach" for £19.95, and "Divorced Barbie" for £299.99.'

The man was shocked and asked, 'Why does the divorced Barbie cost £299.99 when the rest are only £19.95?'

The assistant replied, 'Because "Divorced Barbie" comes with Ken's car, Ken's house, Ken's boat, Ken's furniture, Ken's computer, and one of Ken's friends.'

'I wish I'd listened to what my mother told me.'

'Why, what did she tell you?'

'I don't know. I didn't listen.'

In the old Highlands McTavish awoke early one morning to find his wife had died in the night. With admirable presence of mind, he called out to his servant: 'Maggy, you'll only need to cook the one egg for breakfast this morning.'

Two Scotsmen were walking through a rough part of Glasgow and saw a gang of youths approaching them.

'I think we're going tae get mugged here, Sandy,' said one.

'I think ye're right, Donald,' said the other, passing him a wad of cash. 'Here's that hundred poond I owe ye.'

Customer: (to chemist) I'd like a bar of soap please.

Chemist: Would you like it scented?

Customer: No, I'll take it with me now.

Recent research shows up to 25% of American women are receiving professional therapy for 'shopping addiction'. This is a terrifying statistic, as it shows that the other 75% are going untreated.

Smith: My father was very particular about my education. He wanted me to have all the opportunities he never had.

Jones: Did he send you to Eton?

Smith: No, to a girls' school.

Murphy went for a job on a building site. 'You'll need to be able to make tea and drive a four ton truck,' said the foreman.

'Jaysus,' said Murphy. 'How big is the teapot?!'

First vicar: I keep hearing on the TV adverts that this Christmas will be the greatest ever.

Second vicar: I rather thought that was the first one?

Seamus and Paddy had too much to drink and decided to spend the night at a hotel in Dublin. They asked for a room with two single beds. It was dark and they couldn't find the light switch in the room.

They were so drunk they both got into the same bed without realising. A few seconds later Seamus said 'Paddy, wake up. There's someone in my bed wit me.'

There was a pause and Paddy said 'There's someone in my bed as well!'

'Tell you what Paddy,' said Seamus, 'you tip that feller out of your bed and I'll tip that feller out of my bed!'

So Paddy pushed Seamus out of bed onto the floor.

Seamus howled with pain and said 'Paddy, the one in my bed's only gone and tipped me out before I tipped him out!'

'Sure never mind,' said Paddy. 'You can get in with me!'

'Every night when I go to bed, I think about plumbing.'

'Do you think you'll pursue it as a career?'

'No, it's just a pipe dream.'

'How dare you drink before me!' said the judge to the drunk who had just swigged from a bottle in court. 'I'm sorry yeronnner,' replied the man, passing the bottle to the judge. 'I should have offered you a drink first!'

Quasimodo walked into a pub and ordered a whisky.

'Bell's all right?' asked the barman.

'Don't talk shop,' said Quasimodo.

A man walked into a pub and saw an impressive stuffed bull's head on the wall above the bar. The landlord saw the man looking at it and said 'That bull killed my father.' 'Was he a bull fighter?' asked the man.' No,' replied the landlord. 'He was standing there under it and it fell on him.'

'I know a man who eats nothing but Chinese food.'

'Why's that?'

'He's a Chinaman.'

A drunken husband was singing his wife's praises to the assembled dinner guests. 'My dear wife thinks of everything. Why, to make my life easier, she even installed a special light in the bathroom, which comes on automatically whenever I have to go in the middle of the night.'

The wife gasped with horror. 'So it's YOU that's been peeing in the fridge!'

A toilet has been stolen from a police station in Letchworth, Herts. Police say they have nothing to go on.

A woman was disturbed at breakfast by the bin men outside and realised she'd forgotten to leave her dustbin out on the pavement to be emptied.

She rushed out into the street in her old dressing gown stained with egg, a cigarette end dangling from her mouth and her hair full of curlers, and the remains of a mud mask on her face from the night before.

'Am I too late for the rubbish collection?' she asked.

'No love,' replied the binman. 'Jump in!'

A man walked into a barber's and asked to have his hair cut like David Beckham.

Twenty minutes later the man's hair was chopped unevenly with a ragged fringe and razor nicks around the ears. Disgusted, the man said 'This is awful – David Beckham's hair doesn't look like this!'

'It would if he had it cut in here,' said the barber.

On a beautiful summer's day, two English tourists were driving through Wales.

At Llanfairpwllgwyngyllgogerychwyrndrobwyllllantysiliogogogoch they stopped for lunch and one of the tourists asked the waitress: 'Before we order, I wonder if you could settle an argument for us. Can you pronounce where we are, very, very, very slowly?'

The girl leaned over and said:

'Burrr... gurrr... King.'

A man walked into a hairdresser's and said 'give me a Tony Curtis.'

The barber shaved all the man's hair off and left him totally bald.

When the man looked in the mirror he recoiled in shock. 'Don't you know what Tony Curtis looks like?' he shouted.

'I should do,' said the barber. 'I saw 'The King and I' fourteen times!'

The barber tried to sell me a tortoiseshell comb. I can't imagine what it's for, all the tortoise shells I've seen have been bald.

They say contentment is wealth. But you can't spend it.

'How's your new job?'

'I've got 500 people under me.'

'Sounds important!'

'No, I'm cutting the grass at the cemetery'

A woman took an old photograph of her late mother to a photographer and asked if it could be enlarged. 'Certainly madam', said the photographer, 'come back next Wednesday and it will be ready.' 'There's just one thing' said the woman. 'I never liked that hat she's got on in the picture. Could you take it out?' The photographer looked at the picture and said 'yes, I think we can do that by airbrushing. But I'll need to know what sort of hairstyle she had.' 'Well you'll see that when you take the hat out!' replied the customer.

A few years ago we had Steve Jobs, Bob Hope and Johnny Cash.

Now we have no Jobs, no Hope and no Cash.

A retired couple consulted with an architect to build their dream home.

The wife pointed to the plans. 'This window here means that the neighbours will be able to see me in the shower!' she said in horror.

'Don't worry dear,' said her husband. 'They'll only look once.'

My wife gave me one of those badger shaving brushes for Christmas. I said what do I want to go shaving badgers for?

'Where are you going with your dog?'

'I'm taking him to the vets to have him put down.'

'Is he mad?'

'Well he's not very happy about it.'

A fool and his money are hard to find.

There was a beautiful young woman knocking on my hotel room door all night. I finally had to let her out.

Pupil: 'Who was that lady I seed you with last night?'

Teacher: '"I saw, I saw"'.

Pupil: 'Alright then, who was that eyesore I seed you with last night?'

An elderly lady was describing how she and her husband had met and fallen in love at the old people's home. 'We talked to each other and just clicked,' she said.

'Yes,' added the husband. 'Elbows, knees and hips.'

Wife: How come you never bring me flowers?

Husband: What's the point? They could be dead in a week.

Wife: So could you, but I still like having you around.

The Welsh Guards were surrounded by Zulus. The soldiers fought desperately as the spears flew thick and fast. Young Private Evans stood up and began singing 'Men of Harlech' and more spears flew at them, killing Evans.

Private Jones stood up and began to sing 'All Through the Night'. A spear cut him down instantly.

Private Davies stood up and before he could open his mouth the officer shouted 'For God's sake man sing them something they like!'

Three Welshmen were in a pub praising the beer.

Jones: Best glass of beer I never tasted no better.

Evans: So did I neither.

Davies: 'Neither did I too.

What did Quasimodo get when he retired?

A lump sum and forty years' back pay.

What's the best way to ensure a letter of complaint to Royal Mail gets looked at?

Put it inside a birthday card.

On their silver wedding anniversary the wealthy heiress said to her husband, 'now look me in the eye and tell me honestly, that you didn't marry me for my money.' 'I didn't,' replied her husband, 'but by this time I think I've earned it.'

Definition of old: someone who still remembers when he knew more than his phone.

'Where were you born?'

'London.'

'What part?'

'All of me.'

Two women friends met after many years.

'Tell me,' said one, 'What happened to your son?'

'My son? the poor, poor boy!' sighed the other. 'He unfortunately married a girl who won't do a thing around the house. She won't cook, she won't clean. All she does is lie on the sofa watching TV. The poor boy even has to bring her breakfast in bed, would you believe it?'

'That's really awful!'

'And what about your daughter?'

'Ah, now she's the lucky one! She married an angel. He won't let her do anything in the house. He does all the cooking and cleaning. And each morning he brings her breakfast in bed, would you believe it? Then all she has to do is spend the whole day with her feet up watching TV.'

I think my wife would divorce me, if she could find a way of doing it without making me happy.

A man walked into a bar on the top floor of the hotel he was staying in. He sat down next to a drunk who said; 'you see that window over there? If you jump out you fly back in.'

'Prove it,' the man said. So the drunk dived out the window and flew back in.

The man was amazed and immediately jumped out of the window, fell fifty stories to the pavement and was killed instantly.

The barman looked over and sighed.

'You're a real nuisance when you're drunk, Superman.'

'Where are you going on holiday this year?'

'Spain, in August.'

'Spain in August! You'll hate it. It'll be a hundred degrees in the shade.'

'Well I don't have to stay in the shade, do I?'

'I once knew a man with one leg called Levitsky.'

'What was his other leg called?'

You can tell a lot about a woman from her hands. For instance, if they're placed around your throat, she's probably quite annoyed.

'How was your blind date?'

'Terrible! He showed up in a 1932 Rolls-Royce.'

'What's so terrible about that?'

'He was the original owner.'

My hamster died yesterday. He fell asleep at the wheel.

A tramp knocked on the back door of a large house. The wealthy lady of the house answered the door. 'Yes?' she said imperiously, looking at the shabby visitor.

'Sorry to bother you missus, but I haven't eaten for three days. Could you spare a few pence?'

'I'm sorry,' replied the lady, 'but I don't give money to beggars. However, if you are willing to work, there are one or two jobs that need to be done around the place.'

'Right you are missus,' said the man. 'I'm willing to work fer me keep.'

'Good,' said the lady. She handed him some sandpaper, a tin of paint and a brush. 'Go round to the front of the house and repaint the porch.'

Off went the tramp. An hour later he returned with a big smile on his face and his hand held out. 'I've done the job like you said missus. But by the way, it's not a porch, it's a Ferrari.'

Welshman: I will now sing 'All through the night'.

Englishman: Couldn't you finish a bit earlier?

Enid met her old friend Deirdre at a school reunion.

'My dear,' said Deirdre, 'you haven't changed a bit in forty years!'

'Good Lord,' replied Enid. 'You mean I looked like this forty years ago?'

Stan feared his wife Mavis wasn't hearing as well as she used to and he thought she might need a hearing aid. Not quite sure how to approach her, he called the doctor to discuss the problem.

The doctor told him there was a simple informal test the husband could perform before bothering with a full examination in the surgery.

'Here's what you do,' said the doctor. 'Stand about 20 feet away from her, and in a normal conversational speaking tone see if she hears you. If not, go to 10 feet, then 5 feet, and so on until you get a response.'

That evening, Mavis was in the kitchen cooking dinner and Stan was in the living room, about 20 feet away. He decided to try the test. 'What's for dinner, Mavis?' he said.

No response.

So he moved closer to the kitchen, and repeated 'Mavis, what's for dinner?' Still no response.

Next he moved right into the kitchen, just five feet behind his wife, and said 'Mavis, what's for dinner?'

Again he gets no response.

Finally he walked right up behind her. 'Mavis, what's for dinner?'

'FOR THE FOURTH TIME STAN, IT'S SHEPHERD'S PIE!'

During Sunday service the vicar stood up and said 'It is with great regret that I have to announce that our long standing treasurer, Mr Greenhill, has absconded with the organist's wife and half the church funds.' There was a gasp from the congregation as the clergyman continued. 'We will now sing hymn number 634, 'There is a green hill far away.'

Customer (in restaurant): Waiter, this chicken must be at least ten years old!

Waiter: How can you tell?

Customer: By the teeth.

Waiter: But chickens don't have teeth.

Customer: No, but I do!

Newsflash: a Lancashire woman is suing her local hospital after her husband underwent an operation which she claimed caused him to lose interest in sex. A hospital spokesman said all they had done was perform routine cataract surgery which had improved his eyesight.

A man and his nagging wife went to Honolulu on holiday. Soon they began to argue about the correct way to pronounce the word 'Hawaii.' The man insisted that it was pronounced Hawaii, with a 'w' sound. The wife said it was pronounced like 'Havaii,' with a 'v' sound.

Finally, they saw an old native on the beach, and asked him which was correct. The old man said 'it's "Havaii."'

'You idiot,' the wife said to her husband. 'I told you I was right!' As they left she thanked the old man.

He replied 'you're velcome.'

An eighteenth-century vagabond, exhausted and famished, came to a roadside inn with a sign reading: 'George and the Dragon.' He knocked. The innkeeper's wife stuck her head out a window. 'Could ye spare some victuals?' He asked. The woman glanced at his shabby, dirty clothes. 'No!' she shouted. 'Could I have a pint of ale?' 'No!' she shouted. 'Could I at least sleep in your stable?' 'No!' she shouted again. The vagabond said, 'Might I please...?' 'What now?' the woman screeched, not allowing him to finish. 'D'ye suppose,' he asked, 'that I might have a word with George?'

Evans was watching a rugby game in Cardiff.

In the packed stadium there was only one empty seat, right next to him.

'Whose is that seat?' asked a man in the row behind.

'I got the ticket for my wife,' said Evans. 'But she died in an accident.'

'So you're keeping the seat vacant as a mark of respect?'

'No,' said the fan, 'I offered it to all of my friends.'

'So why didn't they take it?'

'They've all gone to the funeral.'

My wife asked me if I was having an affair with a woman from Llanfairpwllgwyngyllgogerychwyrndrobwyllllatysiliogogogoch.

I said: 'How can you say such a thing?'

The great dramatist J.B. Priestley is said to have attended a performance of one of his plays, but for reasons unknown decided to leave the theatre before the show ended. On hearing this, the lead actor exclaimed 'if that's the way he feels about the play, he shouldn't have written it!'

A man and his wife stayed on a farm one summer.

They enjoyed it but were doubtful about going back there the following year because of the smell of the pig-sty next to the house.

The man wrote to the farmer about it and the farmer replied:

'We haven't had any pigs on the farm since you were here last summer. Do come again.'

Drunk (to barman): Can you recommend a good port?

Barman: Yes – Southampton – there's a train leaving in ten minutes!

A businessman was staying in a small Alpine town for a few days. One night he felt a bit lonely and asked the pub landlord if there were any loose women he could visit.

'They've all been driven out by the new priest,' said the man sadly. 'But one or two are still working in the old cave on the edge of town. All you do is go into the cave and whistle. If you hear a whistle coming back, you're in luck.'

The businessman eagerly went on his way. It was a dark night and he had trouble finding the cave but eventually he got inside and whistled. He was delighted to hear a whistle come back.

Two seconds later he was knocked down by an express train.

I once had a Welsh girlfriend with 36DDs. It was the longest surname I've ever seen.

A Scotsman and an Englishman met in London, both penniless, both thirsty.

The Englishman had an idea for getting a free drink: 'I know a barmaid in a pub near here who has got a very bad memory. If you get her involved in a conversation she can't remember whether you've paid or not. Let me try it on first.'

The Englishman went into the pub and duly got his free drink. Then it was the Scotsman's turn to try.

He went over to the bar, ordered his pint and began to tell the barmaid all about life in the Highlands. Ten minutes later he drained his glass and said to the barmaid:

'Well, it's been nice talking to you but I've got to be off now. What about my change?'

Sergeant (to new army recruit): What would you do if somebody attacked you with a rifle butt?

Recruit: But what?

'My husband's just died, worth a million pounds.'

'Sorry to hear that. Did he leave you much?'

'Oh, about twice a month.'

A man went into a garage and said to the mechanic, 'I need a new 710 cap for my car engine, the old one's broken,'

The mechanic scratched his head. 'I've never heard of one of those. What make is it?'

'A BMW 5 series,' replied the man.

'What's the thing called again?'

'A 710 cap,' replied the man, getting a little impatient. 'Look, I've got it in my pocket.'

He handed a small disk to the mechanic who looked at it for a moment then turned the disk round.

'You've been reading it upside down. That's an OIL cap!'

A Scotsman went into a butcher's and asked for ten pence worth of steak.

Surprised at the small amount, the butcher asked 'ten pence worth of steak? What do you want it for?'

'Five pence.'

A story is told of Sir Noel Coward's reaction after he received some bad press. He wrote to the critic 'I have just read your upsetting review in the smallest room in the house, but I managed to put it all behind me.'

An old man walked into a shoe mender's and said 'In 1939 my father left a pair of shoes here but then he went off to the war and was killed. Have you still got them?'

Thinking it must be a joke, the cobbler laughed. 'Have you got a ticket?'

The man solemnly produced a faded ticket from his wallet and placed it on the counter. 'We found this amongst my mother's things when she died some weeks ago. She'd kept it all these years.'

The cobbler realised the man was serious. He examined the ticket and scratched his head.

'Look sir, this place has changed hands dozens of times since 1939,' he said, 'but I'll see if I can find them.'

He went down to the cellar and rummaged around in the far corners until he finally found the shoes in a cupboard. He emerged from the cellar waving them triumphantly.

'I've found them,' he cried, as he blew the dust off them. 'Ready next Thursday.'

On one occasion, a man making heavy breathing sounds from a phone box told the worried operator: 'I haven't got a pen so I'm steaming up the window to write the number on.'

Marriage isn't a word, it's a sentence.

I went into an electrical shop the other day and asked for a kettle. 'Kenwood?' asked the man. 'Alright then,' I replied, 'where is he?'

First farmer: Do you find it pays to keep a cow?

Second farmer: Oh yes. Mine makes two gallons of milk a day.

First farmer: And how much of that do you sell?

Second farmer: Four gallons.

Two Yorkshiremen were talking in the pub. 'There's a terrible smell in our house,' said Stan.

'Why's that?' said Bert.

'Well,' replied Stan, 'it's the fault of the missus. She keeps her six cats int' front room and they stink t'place out.'

'Canst thou not open t'window in't room?' replied Bert.

'Nay!' said Stan. 'Don't be daft. Then all me pigeons would fly out!'

Doctor: I haven't seen you for a long time.

Patient: I know, I've been ill.

Customer (in pet shop): I want a thousand cockroaches.

Shopkeeper: What on earth do you want them for?

Customer: My tenancy expires today and the contract says I have to leave the house exactly as I found it.

Paddy and Seamus were up from County Kerry on the spree in Dublin and were the worse for wear. They got into a taxi, demanding to be taken to Temple Bar. They slumped forward in their seats, semi-conscious.

The driver didn't want two drunks in his cab and guessed they were too sozzled to know where they were, so instead of moving the vehicle he just revved the engine loudly a few times then switched it off and shouted 'here we are fellers.'

'Thanks a million, that was nice and quick!' said Paddy, and staggered out of the cab, none the wiser. But Paddy stopped, leant through the partition and grabbed the driver by the scruff of his neck.

'What the hell do you tink you're playing at!' he slurred. The taxi driver thought for a moment he'd been rumbled until Paddy continued. 'You drove so fast you could have killed us!'

Woman (to gym instructor): Can you teach me to do the splits?

Gym instructor: How flexible are you?

Woman: I can't do Wednesdays or Fridays.

The definition of 'mixed feelings': seeing your mother in law drive your brand new car over a cliff.

A man walks into a bar with a roll of tarmac under his arm and says: 'Pint please, and one for the road.'

When the inventor of the drawing board messed things up, what did he go back to?

I cleaned the attic with the wife the other day. Now I can't get the cobwebs out of her hair.

Barber (to customer): That'll be ten pounds, sir.

Customer: Ten pounds? Look here, the sign in your window says "High class hair cut, five pounds."'

Barber: I know, but your hair's not high class.

A university teacher wrote these words on the blackboard: 'woman without her man is nothing'. The teacher then asked the students to punctuate the words correctly.

The men wrote: 'Woman, without her man, is nothing.'

The women wrote: 'Woman! Without her, man is nothing.'

While he was visiting his son, an old man asked for the password to the wi-fi.

'It's taped under the keyboard,' said his son.

After three failed attempts to log on, the man asked, 'Am I spelling this right? T-A-P-E-D-U-N-D-E-R-T-H-E-K-E-Y-B-O-A-R-D?

What did they call the boy who finally stood up to the school bully?

An ambulance.

A Scottish minister called on the English couple that had just moved onto a small island in the Hebrides. 'Will you be attending our church this Sunday?' he asked them.

The couple didn't want to go but didn't wish to appear rude.

'Well,' said the husband, 'We'd like to, but the service is in Gaelic.'

'That's alright,' replied the clergyman. 'The collection is in English.'

The phone was ringing so I picked it up and said 'Who's speaking please?' and the caller said 'you are.'

A policeman asked two drunks for their names and addresses. The first answered, 'I'm Paddy O'Riley, of no fixed abode.' The second replied, 'I'm Seamus O'Toole, and I live in the flat above Paddy.'

One dark night a teenager took a shortcut home through the cemetery. Halfway across, he was startled by a tapping noise coming from the misty shadows. Trembling with fear, he saw an old man with a hammer and chisel, chipping away at a headstone.

'I thought you were a ghost,' said the relieved teen. 'What are you doing working so late?'

'Oh, those idiots,' grumbled the old man. 'They misspelt my name!'

A professor was trying to instruct the class in the very important duty of cultivating the faculty of observation. To emphasize his point he mixed a very noxious compound in a basin and then said, 'I want you to all observe what I do and then come forward and do exactly the same thing.'

He dipped his finger into the basin and put it into his mouth, making a very wry face. Each member of the class came to his desk and dipped a finger into the bowl, placed it in the mouth and departed for his seat with a very disgusted expression of countenance.

When all were seated once more the professor said, 'None of you observed what I did, for, had you done so, you would have perceived that the finger I put in my mouth was not the one I dipped into the basin.'

A girl was crying bitterly.

Mother: What happened dear?

Daughter: Mummy do I look like a wicked witch?

Mother: No!

Daughter: Are my eyes all funny?

Mother: No!

Daughter: Is my nose big?

Mother: No dearest!

Daughter: Am I fat?

Mother: You are a beautiful little girl!

Daughter: Then why do people keep telling me I look so much like you?

Husband: I've just seen our daughter knitting baby clothes.

Wife: Thank heavens for that. She's finally started doing something other than chase men around.

Farmer Giles was complaining to a friend about his new bull.'All that bull does is eat grass. Won't even look at a cow.'

'Take him to the vet,' his friend suggested.

The next week, Farmer Giles was much happier. 'The vet gave him some pills, and the bull serviced all of my cows!' he told his friend. 'Then he broke through the fence and bred with all my neighbour's cows!'

'What kind of pills were they?' asked the friend.

'I don't know,' said the farmer,' but they've got a minty taste.'

Doctor: Do you want the good news or the bad news first?

Patient: Give me the good news.

Doctor: You're going to have a disease named after you.

When my wife gets a little upset, sometimes a simple 'Calm down' in a soothing voice is all it takes to get her a lot upset.

Two days before her birthday, a wife said to her husband meaningfully, 'last night I dreamt I received a diamond necklace. What do you suppose that means?'

The husband thought for a moment then said with a smile, 'perhaps you'll find out on your birthday.'

With mounting excitement, the wife opened a package from her husband on her birthday.

Inside was a book entitled 'How to Interpret Dreams.'

'My wife is on a three week diet.'

'How much has she lost so far?'

'Two weeks.'

'I lost my dog last night. What should I do?'

'Put a poster on a tree.'

'Why? He can't read.'

Paddy was at a Dublin specialist for an examination. The nurse handed him a small plastic bottle and told him to urinate in it.

'Sure and not in front of all these people?' said Paddy in a shocked voice.

'Certainly not,' replied the nurse, pointing to the lavatory. 'Do it in that room.'

A few minutes later Paddy emerged and handed the nurse the empty bottle.

'Turns out I didn't need it,' he said. 'There was a toilet in there.'

A politician was on a tour of a psychiatric hospital. He asked the director how they decided if a patient needed to be committed.

'Well,' the director said, 'we fill a bath with water, then offer the patient a teaspoon, a teacup and a bucket, and ask him to empty the tub.'

'I see,' the politician said. 'A normal person would use the bucket because it's the biggest.'

'No,' the director said. 'A normal person would pull the plug.'

Doctor (to receptionist): Have you seen my auroscope?

Receptionist: No! Does it say anything good?

McTavish set up his stall at the car boot sale. After a while he had to answer the call of nature, so asked his friend McDougal at the next stall to mind his things for him.

'Whatever ye do, if someone wants those bagpipes, make sure you get a good price for them.'

'Alright, but if someone wants to haggle, how low are ye willing to go?' asked McDougal.

'Weelll...try for £50, but I'm willing to accept £20.'

A few minutes later McTavish returned and was surprised to see the bagpipes were gone.

'How much did ye get for the bagpipes?' asked McTavish.

'Twenty poond,' replied McDougal.

'Who bought them?'

'I did.'

Smith: Why do you call your car 'Daisy'?

Jones: Well, some days 'e starts, and some days 'e doesn't!

Sunday school teacher: Can anyone tell me what an evangelist is?

Little Johnny: Someone who plays the evangelo.

Bert and Mavis were getting married at the grand old ages of 95 and 94 respectively.

Before the wedding, they visited the local chemist.

'Do you sell heart medication?' asked Bert.

'Of course,' replied the chemist.

'What about pills for arthritis and lumbago?' asked Mavis.

'Certainly,' the chemist said.

'How about corn plasters, surgical stockings and back rests?' enquired Bert.

'Yes, we've got all those,' the chemist said.

'Do you have wheelchairs and zimmer frames?' asked Mavis.

'We've got plenty of those in the back room,' replied the chemist.

'That's great,' said Bert. 'There's just one more question.'

'What's that?' asked the chemist, wondering what on earth more they could require.

'Can we have our wedding list here?'

Who earns a living by driving his customers away?

A taxi driver.

A military man had been posted overseas for five years. He got an early discharge and came back to England, looking forward to seeing his wife and daughter who'd only been a baby when he left. He phoned ahead to tell his wife he'd be arriving home sooner than expected.

'Hello?' said a little girl's voice.

'Hello, it's your Daddy,' said the man. 'Is mummy near the phone?'

'No, Daddy. She's upstairs in the bedroom with Uncle Geoff.' After a brief pause, the man said, 'But you don't have an Uncle Geoff!'

'Yes I do. He's upstairs in the bedroom with Mummy!'

The man thought quickly. ' Here's what I want you to do. Put down the phone, run upstairs, knock on the bedroom door and shout in to Mummy and Uncle Geoff that a man has just opened the front door and he says he's your daddy.'

'Okay, Daddy!'

A few minutes later, the little girl came back to the phone. 'Well, I did what you said, Daddy.'

'And what happened?'

'Well, Mummy jumped out of bed with no clothes on and ran around screaming, then she tripped over the rug and went out the back window and now she's all dead.'

'Oh my god! What about Uncle Geoff?'

'He jumped out of bed with no clothes on too and he was all scared and he jumped out the back window into the river, and now he's dead too.'

There was a long pause, then the man said, 'River? Is this Aylesbury 31227?'

Customer (in chemist's shop): Have you got anything to cure worms?

Chemist: I don't know – what's wrong with them exactly?

What is heavy forwards but not backwards?

Ton

A drunk was eating alone at a restaurant. He ordered the most expensive meal on the menu and called out 'drinks on the house for everybody!' His fellow diners were delighted. Half an hour later he ordered another bottle of champagne for himself and said 'drinks on the house for everybody!' again.

He ran up a huge bill and when it was time to pay, he simply smiled at the waiter and said 'I've got no money!' The waiter was furious and dragged the man into the kitchen, punched him in the face and smashed a frying pan over his head, then pulled him out through the restaurant to the front door. Before he could throw him out the man shouted to the other diners again 'Drinks on the house for everybody!'

Then he turned to the waiter and said 'But not for you – when *you* drink you get nasty!'

Did you hear about the calendar printer? He got fired for taking a day off.

I phoned the local builders today, I said to them 'Can I have a skip outside my house?' He said, 'I'm not stopping you!'

First vicar: What's the difference between a terrorist and an organist?

Second vicar: You can negotiate with a terrorist.

Judge (to defendant): You stand accused of shooting your mother-in-law while drunk. Can't you see the terrible effect alcohol has had on you?

Defendant: I'll say. It made me miss!

Did you hear about the hungry clock? It went back four seconds.

A man walked into a bar and asked for an orange juice.

'Still orange?' said the barman?

'Well I haven't just changed my mind,' replied the man.

Paddy went to London and got talking to a man in a pub. The man said 'I'll bet you a fiver you can't solve this riddle. I'm looking at a portrait of a man and I say 'Brothers and sisters have I none, but that man's father is my father's son.' Who's the man in the picture?'

Paddy thought for a long while. 'Ah bejaysus,' he said 'sure and that's a difficult one. Here's the five pounds, I give up, what's the answer?'

'I'm looking at a picture of myself,' replied the man.

Paddy was impressed and decided he'd try this one out when he got home. So back in Dublin he met his old pal Seamus and said 'You'll never solve this one. I'm looking at a portrait of a man and I says to meself, 'Brothers and sisters have I none, but that man's father is my father's son.' Who's the man in the picture?'

'Sure and that's easy, I've heard this one before!' said Seamus. 'It's you!'

'That's where you're wrong!' cried Paddy. 'It's a feller I met in a pub in London!'

Hiker (to girl struggling to lead a cow): Where are you going with that cow?

Girl: Taking her to the bull.

Hiker: Can't the farmer do that?

Girl: Oh no, it has to be the bull.

Patient: I'm very worried about my brother, doctor. He thinks he's an orange.

Psychiatrist: Well you'd better fetch him here and I'll examine him.

Patient: There's no need, doctor. I've got him here in my pocket!

When the gorilla died in the zoo, the zookeeper hired a student to put on an ape costume and act like a gorilla until he could find a new one.

In his cage, the student pranced about, made noises and generally threw himself into the part, drawing a big crowd. He then climbed onto the fence of the neighbouring lion's cage, infuriating the animal. Suddenly he lost his footing and fell into the lion's den.

Terrified, the student shouted for help. The lion pounced, opened its jaws and whispered, 'Shut up! Do you want to get us both fired?!'

A husband and wife had been married for 50 years. The woman kept in the wardrobe a shoe box that she forbade her husband from ever opening. But when she was on her deathbed she asked him to open the box.

Inside was a knitted tea cosy and £20,000 in cash.

'My mother told me that the secret to a happy marriage was to never argue,' she explained. 'Instead, I should keep quiet and knit a tea cosy.'

Her husband was touched. Only one tea cosy was in the box—that meant she'd been angry with him only once in 50 years. 'But what about all this money?' he asked.

'Oh,' she said, 'that's the money I made from selling the tea cosies.'

Wife: You loved me before we were married.

Husband: Well, now it's your turn!

'I once knew an eccentric artist who painted a cobweb on the wall. It was so realistic that the cleaning lady spent three hours trying to clean it off.'

'Sorry, I don't believe it.'

'Well, artists are like that sometimes.'

'Yes, but cleaning ladies aren't.'

Coroner: What were your husband's last words?

Widow: 'I don't see how they can make a profit on vodka that costs 99p a bottle.'

Baby flower: Mummy, how did I get made?

Mummy flower: Why, the stalk brought you!

Customer(in chemist's shop): I'd like some talcum powder please.

Assistant: Certainly sir. Walk this way please.

Customer: If I could walk that way I wouldn't need the talcum powder!

'I'm going to the doctors, I don't like the look of my wife.'

'I'll come with you, I hate the sight of mine.'

Jones: I went out with a blonde the other day and she made me dizzy.

Smith: How's that?

Jones: Before I knew it I'd lost my bank balance.

'I don't know her to speak to, only to speak about.'

Definition of junk: something you keep for ten years and then throw away two weeks before you need it.

There are some people so addicted to exaggeration that they can't even tell the truth without lying.

'How was the bridge party last night?'

'It was fine until the police came and looked under the bridge!'

'The ball glanced off my head into the wicketkeeper's hands,' said the batsman on returning to the pavilion, 'and that fool of an umpire gave me out.' 'Well,' observed a teammate, 'sometimes they go by sound.'

Sign on spiritualist medium's front door: 'Please ring bell, as knocking can cause confusion.'

'Are your relatives in business?'

'Yes – in the iron and steel business'

'Oh, indeed?'

'Yes – me mother irons and me father steals'

A drunk phoned the police to report that thieves had been in his car. 'They've stolen the dashboard, the steering wheel, the brake pedal, even the accelerator,' he cried. 'Oh hang on,' he added. 'I'm in the back seat.'

Tourist (to pub landlord): When does the Loch Ness monster appear?

Landlord: Usually after six, sir.

Tourist: Six am or six pm?

Landlord: Six whiskies, sir.

I took my wife out for tea and biscuits the other day. It was alright but she didn't like the bit where she had to give blood.

Passenger: Is this the Barking bus?

Driver: No, it just goes 'toot toot!'

Paddy saw a piece of paper sticking to the top of a pillar box but it was too high to read, so he clambered up to the top. When he got to the paper, he saw that it said 'Wet Paint'.

A man went into a public convenience and sat down in one of the cubicles.

A voice from the next cubicle said 'Hi, how are you?'.

Embarrassed, the man said, 'I'm fine, thank you'.

The voice said 'So what are you up to?'

The man replied, 'Just doing the same as you - sitting here!'

The voice said 'Can I come over?'

By this time the man was annoyed and said 'I'm rather busy right now'.

Then the voice said, 'Listen, there's some idiot in the next cubicle answering all my questions. I'll have to call you back'.

Surgeon (to patient): Why are you so nervous?

Patient: Well doctor, it's my first operation.

Surgeon: Really? It's mine as well, but I feel fine.

Husband: Why can't you spend less on clothes? Just buy one good outfit and you'll save money.

Wife: That's just what I've been doing. I buy one good outfit every week.

A store that sells new husbands has opened in New York City , where a woman may go to choose a husband.

The entrance has a description of how the store operates:

You may visit this store ONLY ONCE! There are six floors and the value of the products increase as the shopper ascends the flights. The shopper may choose any item from a particular floor, or may choose to go up to the next floor, but you cannot go back down except to exit the building!

So, a woman went to the Husband Store to find a husband. On the first floor the sign on the door read:

Floor 1 – These men have jobs

She was intrigued, but continued to the second floor, where the sign read:

Floor 2 – These men have jobs and love kids.

'That's nice,' she thought , 'but I want more.' So she continued upwards.

The third floor sign read:

Floor 3 – These men have jobs, love kids, and are extremely good looking.

'Wow,' she thought, but kept going. She went to the fourth floor and the sign read:

Floor 4 – These men have jobs, love kids, are drop-dead good looking and help with housework.

'Oh, mercy me!' she exclaimed, 'I can hardly stand it!' Still, she went to the fifth floor and the sign read:

Floor 5 – These men have jobs, love kids, are drop-dead gorgeous, help with housework, and have a strong romantic streak.

Shewas tempted to stay, but she went to the sixth floor, where the sign read:

Floor 6 – You are visitor 31,456,012 to this floor. There are no men on this floor. This floor exists solely as proof that women are impossible to please. Thank you for shopping at the Husband Store.

Police constable: Madam, I must ask you to accompany me to the station.

Woman: Why, what have I done?

Police constable: Nothing, I'm just a bit scared of the dark.

'I made a small fortune betting on the horses today.'

'So why do you look so unhappy?'

'Because I started with a large fortune.'

A policeman stopped a drunk woman in the street. 'You're staggering,' he said. The woman looked him up and down. 'You're not so bad yourself, dear,' she replied.

Son (to father): Dad, are all married people unhappy?

Father: No son. Just the men.

I went to see my lawyer but he said he was very busy finishing a big case. Turned out there were only two bottles left.

The postman arrived at a little pub in Scotland and said to the landlord, 'Aye, but it's an awfy long hot walk up the hill here, and mighty thirsty work.' Taking the hint, the landlord poured him a glass of whisky. 'Where's the letters then?' asked the landlord. 'Oh there's no letters,' replied the postman, sipping the whisky, 'but it's still an awfy long hot walk up the hill.'

Editor (to new journalist): You should write so that the most ignorant person can understand what you mean.

Journalist: Well, what part of my copy don't you understand?

A man was talking to his girlfriend about his firm's cricket team. 'Jones is coming along nicely. In a few weeks he'll be our best man.'

'Oh darling,' said his girlfriend. 'What a lovely way to ask me.'

Husband: Come along dear, we'll be late for our appointment.

Wife: Don't be so impatient! I've been telling you for the last hour I'll only be five minutes.

Woman (to fiancé) Have you spoken to the vicar about the wedding banns?

Man: We can't afford bands. We'll just have a disco instead.

A railway worker pocketed a tip from a passenger after helping him with his suitcase. The passenger said 'Do you know who I am?' 'No sir,' replied the porter. 'I'm the general manager of this railway,' continued the man. 'Don't you know it's clearly stated in the rule book that you can't take tips from passengers?' 'Yes sir,' replied the quick-thinking porter. 'But there's nothing that says I can't take a present from a colleague.'

McTavish looked depressed, so his friend McGregor asked what the trouble was. 'Mon,' said McTavish, 'I just walked ten miles to see the Cup Final.' 'Wheesht man,' replied McGregor. 'Think of the money ye saved on bus fares!' 'Aye, I know,' said McTavish. 'But by the time I got tae the stadium, I was too tired tae climb over the fence.'

Animal rights activist (to small boy): is that your mother over there in that fur coat?

Boy: Yes.

Activist: Don't you know a poor creature had to suffer to provide that coat?

Boy: Yes. It was Daddy.

McDougal was describing to McTavish how he'd been rescued from drowning in the loch. 'And then, just before they pulled me oot, ma whole life flashed before ma eyes, like a long line o' pictures!' 'Is that so?' replied McTavish with interest. 'Ye didnae happen tae see a picture o' me lending ye a five pound note in 1957, did ye?'

Other titles from Montpelier Publishing

Available from Amazon

Humour and puzzles

The Book of Church Jokes

After Dinner Laughs

After Dinner Laughs 2

Scottish Jokes

Welsh Jokes

The Bumper Book of Riddles, Puzzles and Rhymes

Wedding Jokes

A Little Book of Limericks

The Father Christmas Joke Book for Kids

Men's interest

The Pipe Smoker's Companion

Advice to Gentlemen

The Frugal Gentleman

The Men's Guide to Frugal Grooming

The Real Ale Companion

The Cigar Collection

17695813R00028

Printed in Great Britain
by Amazon